Ready
Text Coll

SAVVAS
LEARNING COMPANY

ISBN-13: 978-0-328-85796-8
ISBN-10: 0-328-85796-3
10 20

Learning About Each Other and the World

APPLE PIE 4th OF JULY

JANET S. WONG

PICTURES BY
Margaret Chodos-Irvine

Seven days a week,
fifty-two weeks,
three hundred sixty-four days a year
(and three hundred sixty-five in a leap year),
our store is open.

Christmas is the only day we close.

Even on Thanksgiving we open the store.
Even on New Year's Day.
Even today, the Fourth of July.

7

I hear the parade coming this way—
boom, boom, boom.

I smell apple pie
in Laura's oven upstairs
and—

PULL

9

chow mein in our kitchen.
Chow mein!
Chinese food
on the Fourth of July?

No one wants Chinese food
on the Fourth of July, I say.

Fireworks are Chinese, Father says,
and hands me a pan full of sweet-and-sour pork.

10

I hear the parade—

12

BOOM, BOOM, BOOM.

I hear the parade passing by.

13

Noon, and customers come
for soda and potato chips.

15

One o'clock,
and they buy ice cream.

Two o'clock.
The egg rolls are getting hard.

Four o'clock,
and the noodles
feel like shoelaces.

Three o'clock.
Ice and matches.

18

No one wants Chinese food
on the Fourth of July, I say.
Mother piles noodles on my plate.

My parents do not understand all American things.
They were not born here.

Even though my father has lived here
since he was twelve,
even though my mother loves apple pie,
I cannot expect them to know

                                 Americans
do not eat Chinese food
on the Fourth of July.

So, I straighten the milk and the videos
and sample a few new candy bars

until five o'clock,

when two hungry customers walk inside
for some Chinese food to go.

I tell them no one—no one—came,
so we ate it up ourselves

but they smell food in the kitchen
now—

and Mother walks through the swinging door
holding a tray of chicken chow mein,

and Father follows her step for step
with a brand-new pan of sweet-and-sour pork—

25

26

and three more people get in line,
eleven more at six o'clock,
nine at seven,
twelve by eight,

27

more and more and more and more

until it's time to close the store—

time to climb to our rooftop chairs,
way up high, beyond the crowd,

where we sit
and watch the fireworks show—

and eat
our apple pie.

Clothes
in Many Cultures

by Heather Adamson

Clothes to Wear

Around the world, everyone wears clothes for work or play.

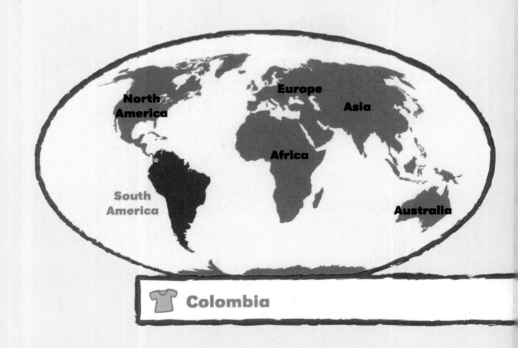

North America

Europe

Asia

Africa

South America

Australia

👕 Colombia

Parkas keep people warm
on cold days.

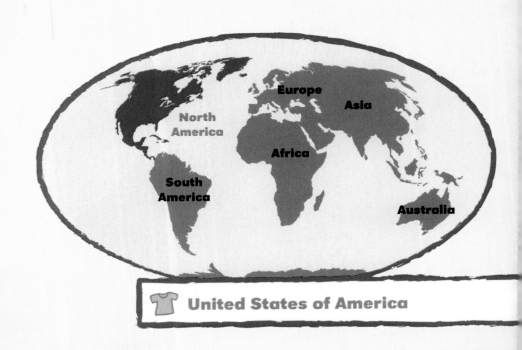

North
America

Europe

Asia

Africa

South
America

Australia

United States of America

Sarongs keep people cool
on hot days.

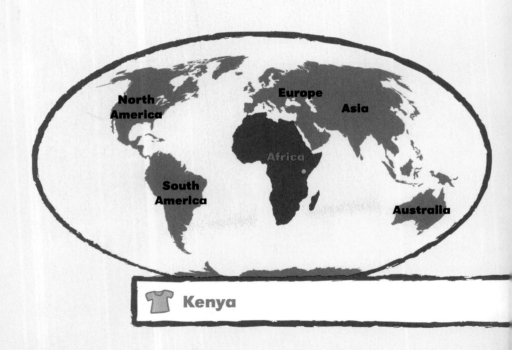

🎽 Kenya

39

Work Clothes

Office workers wear
business suits to their jobs.

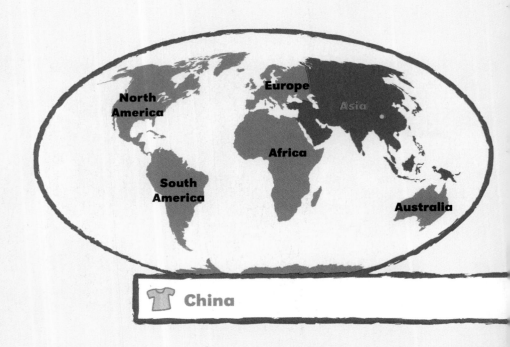

North
America

Europe

Asia

Africa

South
America

Australia

👕 China

40

Traditional Clothes

Brides and grooms wear
fancy clothes
on their wedding day.

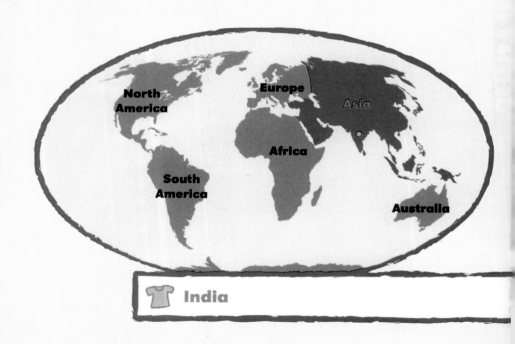

North
America

Europe

Asia

Africa

South
America

Australia

👕 India

45

American Indians wear
bright colors to dance
at powwows.

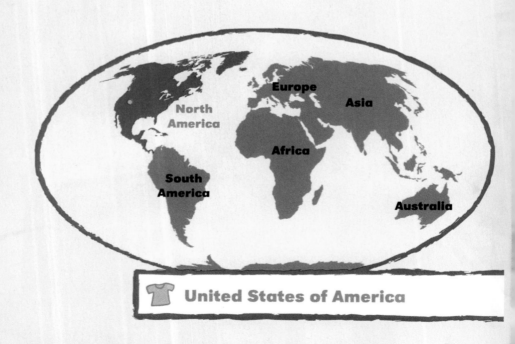

North
America

Europe

Asia

Africa

South
America

Australia

United States of America

47

Scottish men wear
kilts in parades
and at ceremonies.

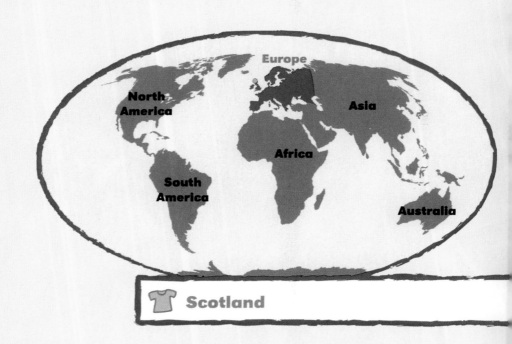

North
America

Europe

Asia

South
America

Africa

Australia

👕 Scotland

49

Your Clothes

Clothes are different
around the world.
What did you wear today?

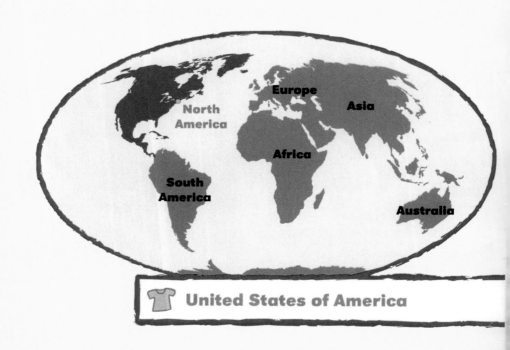

North
America

Europe

Asia

Africa

South
America

Australia

United States of America

GRANDMAS AND GRANDPAS
by Mary Ann Hoberman

My grandma's face is rosy red;
She wears a scarf around her head;
And when she tucks me into bed,
She plants three kisses on my head.

And in the spring she always makes
A garden which she hoes and rakes;
She rubs my tummy when it aches
And bakes me special birthday cakes.

52

My other grandma's face is pale;
She sends me letters in the mail;
She taught me how to play the scale,
And once she wrote a fairy tale.

She knits me mittens, scarves, and socks;
She helps build castles with my blocks;
And when I got the chicken pox,
She let me have her button box.

My grandpa's fat but not too fat;
He likes to wear a cowboy hat;
He tells my grandma's cat to scat
(My grandma doesn't much like that).

He tells me stories that are true
Of all the things he used to do;
Sometimes he takes me to the zoo;
He's teaching me to yodel, too.

My other grandpa's thin and tall,
Which makes him good at basketball.
He visits us each spring and fall
And takes me walking in the mall.

We pick out things we'd like to own,
Like sailboats or a saxophone;
And when we're tired to the bone,
He treats me to an ice-cream cone.

The Crayon Box That Talked

by Shane DeRolf

While walking in a toy store,
The day before today . . .
I overheard a crayon box,
With many things to say.

"I don't like Red!" said Yellow,
And Green said, "Nor do I!
And no one here likes Orange,
But no one knows just why."

"We are a box of crayons
That doesn't get along."
Said Blue to all the others,
"Something here is wrong!"

Well, I bought that box of crayons,
And took it home with me,
And laid out all the colors
So the crayons could all see . . .

They watched me as I colored,
With Red and Blue and Green,
And Black and White and Orange,
And every color in between.

57

They watched as Green became the grass
And Blue became the sky.
The Yellow sun was shining bright
On White clouds drifting by.

Colors changing as they touched,
Becoming something new.
They watched me as I colored.
They watched till I was through.

And when I'd finally finished,
I began to walk away.
And as I did, the crayon box
Had something more to say . . .

"I do like Red!" said Yellow.
And Green said, "So do I!
And, Blue, you were terrific,
So high up in the sky!"

"We are a box of crayons,
Each one of us unique.
But when we get together . . .

The picture is complete."

59

It's a Small World

by Richard M. and Robert B. Sherman

It's a world of laughter, a world of tears.
It's a world of hopes and a world of fears.
There's so much that we share,
That it's time we're aware
It's a small world after all.

It's a small world after all.
It's a small world after all.
It's a small world after all.
It's a small, small world.

There is just one moon and one golden sun.
And a smile means friendship to everyone.
Though the mountains divide,
And the oceans are wide
It's a small world after all.

It's a small world after all.
It's a small world after all.
It's a small world after all.
It's a small, small world.

Kids

by Bobbi Katz

Some of us have black hair.
Some have blond or brown.
Some of us are city kids.
Some live in a small town.
Some of us ride buses.
Some walk to school each day.
Some of us like studying.
Some only want to play.
Some of us are quiet kids.
Some love making noise.
We're every color, shape, and size.
We're girls and we are boys.
Some are learning English.
And that's quite hard to do.
(What makes it even harder,
is if kids laugh at you.)

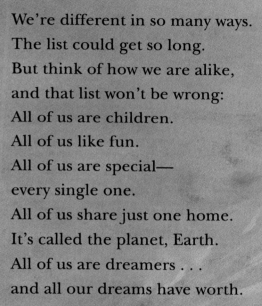

We're different in so many ways.
The list could get so long.
But think of how we are alike,
and that list won't be wrong:
All of us are children.
All of us like fun.
All of us are special—
every single one.
All of us share just one home.
It's called the planet, Earth.
All of us are dreamers . . .
and all our dreams have worth.

63

Text

Apple Pie 4th of July, by Janet S. Wong, pictures by Margaret Chodos-Irvine. Text copyright © 2002 by Janet S. Wong. Illustrations copyright © 2002 by Margaret Chodos-Irvine. Reprinted by permission of Houghton Mifflin Harcourt Publishing Company. All rights reserved.

Excerpted from *Clothes in Many Cultures,* by Heather Adamson. Copyright © 2008 by Capstone. All rights reserved.

"Grandmas and Grandpas," from *Fathers, Mothers, Sisters, Brothers: A Collection of Family Poems* by Mary Ann Hoberman, illustrated by Marylin Hafner. Text copyright © 1991 by Mary Ann Hoberman. Illustrations copyright © 1991 by Marylin Hafner. Used by permission of Little, Brown and Company. All rights reserved. Audio used by permission of The Gina Maccoby Literary Agency. Copyright © 1991 by Mary Ann Hoberman.

The Crayon Box That Talked, by Shane DeRolf. Text copyright © 1996, 1997 by Shane DeRolf. Used by permission of Random House Children's Books, a division of Random House LLC. All rights reserved. Any third party use of this material, outside of this publication, is prohibited. Interested parties must apply directly to Random House LLC for permission.

"It's A Small World," words and music by Richard M. Sherman and Robert B. Sherman. Copyright © 1963 by Wonderland Music Company, Inc. All rights reserved. Published by Hal Leonard Inc.

"Kids," from *Could We Be Friends? Poems for Pals* by Bobbi Katz, illustrated by Joung Un Kim. Copyright © 1997. Published by Mondo Publishing.

Illustrations
56–59 John Nez, **60–61** Paul Eric Roca

Photographs
35 Margie Politzer/Getty Images; **37** Michael Sewell/Peter Arnold Collection/Getty Images; **39** J Marshall/Tribaleye Images/Alamy; **41** Blue Jean Images/Alamy; **43** WorldFoto/Alamy; **45** Baldev Kapoor/Superstock; **47** Chuck Place/Alamy; **49** Tim Graham/Alamy; **51** Elena Elisseeva/Shutterstock.